A BEAUTIFUL HAWAIIAN Day

STORY BY

HENRY KAPONO

PAINTINGS BY

SUSAN SZABO

MUTUAL PUBLISHING

Published by Mutual Publishing

ISBN 1-56647-346-2

First Printing, October 2000
Second Printing, April 2002
2 3 4 5 6 7 8 9

Design by Jane Hopkins

Mutual Publishing
1215 Center Street, Suite 210
Honolulu, Hawaii 96816
Ph: (808) 732-1709
Fax: (808) 734-4094
e-mail: mutual@lava.net
www.mutualpublishing.com

Printed in Korea

ACKNOWLEDGMENTS

Special thanks to my beautiful daughters Ku'umomi and Kaleo, who have brought a joyous light into my life, changing it in many wonderful ways. Both of you have and will always inspire the child in me to create things that bring joy to others. To my Mom & Dad for nurturing and loving the child that I was and will forever be—God bless you and I love you. To my beautiful wife Lezlee, who puts up with the child in me with understanding, dignity, honesty and unconditional love. This story is for all of you.

To Susan Szabo—your heart, imagination, sensitivity and colors have brought such an awesome life and beauty to this story—you are wonderful and surely gifted. To Steve Szabo—your support, positive energy and gracious nature has made this project a very pleasant experience—thank you!

To the readers—I hope your experience is as delightful as it was for us, and that the child in you or the child that you are makes all your dreams come true—Thank you and no matter where you are, always have "A beautiful Hawaiian day!"

—HENRY KAPONO

Many people have contributed to my growth in expressing myself through art and to the joy I experience in creating it. They're too numerous to mention here, but you all know who you are and I love and appreciate all you've given me.

I especially want to thank my mother, Rickey, for igniting and nurturing my love of books and art and my mother-in-law, Betty, for her love and support.

Thank you Steve for being such a faithful friend, inspiring teacher and loving husband. As my soul mate, you enrich my life on all levels.

Mahalo to my fabulous models Kekamalei, Jeremy, Sheana & Corrina. And Mahalo nui loa to Henry for writing such a lovely story and for seeing my art as a visual expression of your words.

—SUSAN SZABO

"Aloooo-ha," said Kaleo, a beautiful Hawaiian girl, as she smiled upon the break of another beautiful Hawaiian day. Beautiful indeed, but no ordinary day for Kaleo.

As
she joyfully
played along the
shoreline, Kaleo noticed
something glowing in the sand—a
sea shell, but not like any she had ever
seen before. She picked it up and admired its
beauty, then, she put the sea shell to her ear,
closed her eyes and heard the most beautiful
sound…

Suddenly, someone grabbed her as a wooden spear drove itself into the very spot she was standing upon.

"Hele mai! Come with me!" said the stranger, and they both ran.

A short time later, she found herself in a dark and damp cave... They quietly listened to the sound of voices and footsteps hurrying by.

"Where am I?" asked Kaleo. The boy spoke in his native tongue, and to her surprise, she understood every word he said.

Knowing
they were safe,
the boy took
her to a very
secret place where
he and his mother
lived. It was a beautiful
place and Kaleo felt very
welcome there.

"Aloha!" said the boy's mama. "Hele
mai! Come with me!" she said. She prepared a
delicious meal of fish and poi, Kaleo's favorite.

They talked for hours into the night
and Kaleo learned so much about
love and respect for the land,
the ocean, the sky and for
one another.

Early the next
morning, the boy
packed a lunch and took
Kaleo hiking. He took her to
his favorite spot at the very top of
a steep and majestic cliff. There she
saw a World more beautiful than she
could ever imagine.

"Wow," she said, as she embraced
the beauty of everything before her. "I
feel like I can touch the sky...and the
ocean...I've never imagined it being
so grand—and the land glows with
all the vibrant colors of the rainbow."

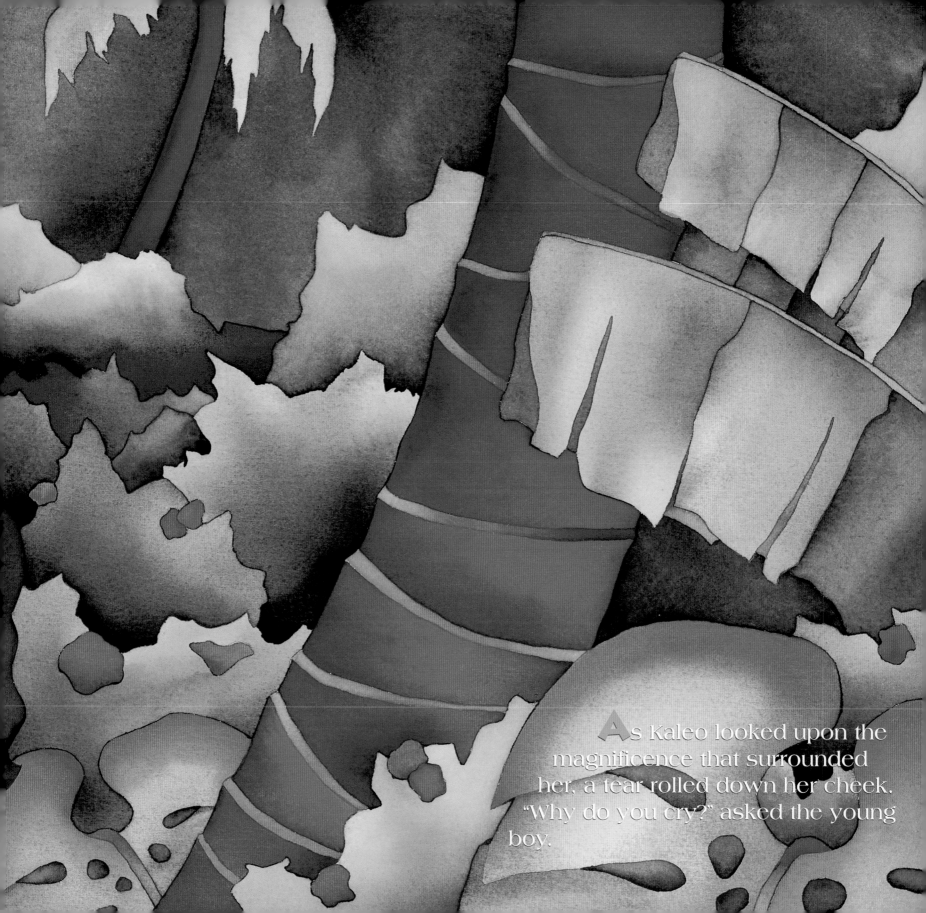

As Kaleo looked upon the magnificence that surrounded her, a tear rolled down her cheek. "Why do you cry?" asked the young boy.

Kaleo told the boy about her home and all the tall buildings, the pollution, the homeless, the crime and all the things she did not see here.

As they talked about her home, Kaleo started to think of her Mom and Dad and her older sister.

"This is a beautiful place," said Kaleo, "and I could stay here forever, but without my family, my life would not be complete. How will I ever get home?"

The boy, understanding her longing, took her by the hand and said, "Hele mai. Come with me."

He took her to a sacred place where two waterfalls gracefully cascade into a pond that empties out into the ocean. The boy told her the legend of the waterfalls and that they represented eternal love.

Then the boy dove into the pond and came out holding the glowing sea shell that had brought Kaleo to this wonderful place.

"This sea shell belongs here," the boy said, "and because of you it is back in its rightful place. Your rightful place is at home with your family. I will dearly miss you. I have learned so much from you. When I am King of all the Islands, I will teach my people to honor this land we call Hawai'i and to love one another. You must do the same," said the boy.

The boy took his kukui nut necklace off and put it around Kaleo's neck.

"This is my gift to you—it represents great knowledge," said the boy.

"It is time for you to go now…I will hold this sea shell to your heart…you must close your eyes and always remember this place and remember me by these words—

Ua mau ke ea o ka aina i ka pono— May the life of the land be perpetuated in righteousness," said the boy. "One day you will know who I am."

Kaleo thought to herself, "Where have I heard that before?"

She kissed him goodbye and closed her eyes and she heard the boy say, "Aloha Kaleo, aloha."

"Can I open my eyes now?"
asked Kaleo.

"Kaleo, where have you
been?" a voice spoke.

Kaleo opened her eyes.
"Momi!" she said. It was
her older sister. She
jumped with joy and said,
"I'm so happy to be home, and I
have much to do and so much to tell
everyone!"

Then she exclaimed,
"Mahalo nui loa, for this day
is most definitely...A Beautiful
Hawaiian Day!"

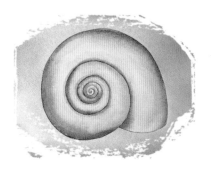

THE END